THE
MOZAMBIQUE
STORY

THE MOZAMBIQUE STORY

Frank Howie

NAZARENE PUBLISHING HOUSE
Kansas City, Missouri

10   9   8   7   6   5   4   3   2   1

TO
HEATHER,
a gracious and loving wife,
a selfless and caring missionary

Rev. Frank Howie has served as a missionary to the People's Republic of Mozambique, Africa, since 1964. He was born in Belfast, Northern Ireland, and received his education from British Isles Nazarene College in Manchester, England.

During his early years in Mozambique, Rev. Howie lived on the Tavane Mission Station, where he was involved in district work and taught several courses in the Bible school. He then went to live in Maputo, where he started the church's first Theological Education by Extension program in Mozambique. Since 1974 he has served as mission director of the Mozambique Mission Council. In addition to administrative duties, he does translation work, develops Portuguese and Shangaan literature, serves as consultant to the Mozambique superintendents, and is active in evangelism among the Mozambique migrant workers in the Republic of South Africa.

Rev. Howie's wife, Heather, a nurse, has served with him the entire tenure in Mozambique. The Howies have two married children who reside with their respective families in Africa.

Contents

Preface

Much of what I have written in this book is based on my personal experience and knowledge of Mozambique and of the Church of the Nazarene in that country. Some of the more detailed information has been gathered from the very considerable amount of correspondence I receive from Mozambicans, from recordings I have taped specifically for this book, as well as from notes taken during discussions with different people.

But most of the events recorded here, the pictures painted, the asides given, are more "unstudied." If I may paraphrase the words of John, they are what I myself have heard, seen with my eyes, have looked at, and my hands have touched. In those cases where I have not had any direct involvement, I have still drawn on my own background knowledge to fill in essential details. If, through this approach, I can convey to you, the reader, something of the atmosphere of the Mozambique scene, as I have experienced it, and something of the excitement of the Lord's work there, as I have felt it, then my purpose will have been fulfilled.

It would be difficult, if not impossible, to really understand the current situation in Mozambique without some understanding of the events that have taken place there in the past number of years. A sense of continuity is essential. Recent Mozambique history has been characterized by dramatic—and often traumatic—changes. These changes have made Mozambique what it is today and have deeply affected the life of the church. Changes are still taking place, even as I write these lines. So I have sometimes "glanced over my shoulder" at past events, to help with an understanding of present ones.

I would like to record my appreciation for my fellow Mozambique missionaries, both past and present. Although their names may not all appear in this book, I have been reminded of them again and again in the writing of it. I have also been reminded of their contribution to the Mozambique work. As for the Mozambicans themselves, whose lives have been so intertwined with mine for so many years, I will let the following chapters speak on my behalf. They will tell of the deep appreciation I have for them, of the great respect in which I hold them. This is their story—the Mozambique story.

▶▶ 1 ◀◀

The Turn
of the Tide

It is the year 1961, and the Portuguese are still the colonial power in Mozambique.

The scene is the Tavane Mission Station, in the southern part of the country. Tavane was the main station of the Church of the Nazarene in that southeast African country. The atmosphere is tense. A man of commanding presence rises to his feet to address a packed gathering of Nazarene nationals and missionaries. Everyone is conscious of the Portuguese security men outside—wary, watchful, alert. The man who is about to speak is Eduardo Mondlane. To the Mozambicans, he is the leader of Frelimo, the Front for the Liberation of Mozambique, hero of the independence struggle. To the Portuguese, he is the leader of a terrorist movement, archenemy of the state.

By a strange irony, Mondlane—who would later be assassinated—has come to Mozambique in his capacity as a United Nations representative. The Portuguese have felt obliged to show their magnanimity to the world by permitting him to enter the colony and to visit places of his choice. He chooses, among other places, the Nazarene main station at Tavane.

Eduardo Mondlane casts his eye out upon the great gathering of people. He singles out the missionaries present. He addresses his next words directly to them. "The time is coming," he says, "when we will take over this country. But before that time comes there will be trouble, great trouble. Like everybody else, you missionaries will be caught up in these troubles. You will have to leave the country. When that time comes, go. But don't be afraid. Because, when all the fighting is over, and the country has been liberated, you will be able to come back again. And you will be welcome."

* * *

Trouble did come, as Eduardo Mondlane said it would. One of the missionaries present at that historic meeting in 1961 was Mozambique Mission Director Armand Doll. Little did anyone know, on that occasion, that Armand would later be imprisoned by the new Marxist government that would come to power in June of 1975. In that year of independence, the missionaries had to leave Mozambique, leaving two of their missionary colleagues in prison. One cannot help but feel that Dr. Mondlane—who received his early education in Mozambique mission schools and who studied and taught in the United States—would have been deeply saddened by such a turn of events.

The national Christians were alone. They were without missionaries, mission support, or financial help from the international church. What would happen to them now, these Mozambican Nazarenes?

The Marxist era had begun.

* * *

It was inevitable that the Tavane Mission Station would be nationalized—confiscated, without compensation—by the authorities. The missionaries had already left. The nationals were the only ones left on the station. Then they, too, were ordered to vacate all the buildings they had been using. They were ordered to hand over the keys of the missionary homes in which they had been living.

"We had nowhere to sleep that night," recalled District

The Tavane Mission Station church before it was nationalized

Superintendent Langa. "But at that time the main station church had not yet been taken. So I gathered all our people together in the evening and led them into the church, to pass the night there."

The men were to sleep on the benches on one side of the church, the women on the other, and the children along the aisle. But before they settled down for the night, Rev. Langa called everybody around the altar. He read the Scriptures. And they sang a hymn:

> *All the way my Saviour leads me.*
> *What have I to ask beside?*
> *Can I doubt His tender mercy*
> *Who thro' life has been my Guide?*
> *Heav'nly peace, divinest comfort,*
> *Here by faith in Him to dwell!*
> *For I know, whate'er befall me,*
> *Jesus doeth all things well.*

"Whate'er befall me." Much was yet to befall them in the following years of the Marxist era. The Savior would lead them, but it would not be easy.

* * *

The Tavane main station church was the last mission building to be taken.

It was a Saturday, the day when old Mother Muiocha was to be buried. The church bells were rung, as was the custom, calling the people to come to the mission. When the bells fell silent, they were destined never to ring again for the purpose of calling people to worship. The funeral service was held in the church—the last meeting to be held there. The sanctuary was filled to capacity. It was a somber and sad service. The congregation mourned the death of Mother Muiocha. They also wept at the loss of their church.

"When the service was over," wrote one of those present, "the doors were closed. We were shut out of the church. But we continue in prayer as we have always done."

You can take the Christians out of the church, and confiscate their buildings, but you cannot take the spirit of prayer out of their hearts.

* * *

A Mozambique missionary came back from furlough toward the end of 1975 and was unable to go back into Mozambique. He wrote the following poignant letter to Nazarene friends overseas:

It seems incredible that so many things could happen in so short a time. Yet it is only a matter of months since we were with you for deputation services. We hope you have not forgotten our words, our appeal for prayer on behalf of Mozambique.

It is so easy to forget after the missionary has gone, there are so many other things that clamor for our time and attention. It is so easy to forget his words, the inspiration of the meetings and their impact upon us—and the solemn promises that were made to him. He called upon us to pray for Mozambique in the critical days that lay ahead for that newly independent country, and we said that we would. And we meant it.

But we must not forget. Not now, of all times. God's people in Mozambique need our prayers; we must not fail them. We must pray and work until the door to Mozambique opens up once again, until the Mozambique church finally emerges from its dark night of testing—a living church, and a triumphant one.

The Nazarene family around the world did not fail its family members in Mozambique. It did not forget to pray. And, in the fullness of time, God answered prayer. The door to that country would open up once again. The church would emerge from its time of testing: leaner, stronger, more victorious than ever before in its history.

We are hard pressed on every side, but not crushed;
perplexed, but not in despair;
persecuted, but not abandoned;
struck down, but not destroyed.
We always carry around in our body the death of Jesus,
so that the life of Jesus
may also be revealed in our body.
For we who are alive are always given over to death
for Jesus' sake,
so that his life may be revealed in our mortal body.
2 Cor. 4:8-11

* * *

It was April 1981. A Nazarene missionary had finally obtained a visa to visit the church in Mozambique. It was the first time a missionary had returned to the country since the Marxist revolution. I drove into the city of Maputo, to an ecstatic welcome from the Mozambican Nazarenes. It had been six years.

"We knew you would come," said Seraque, one of our youth workers. "We knew that our missionaries were just across the border from us, in South Africa, ministering to our Mozambicans who work in the gold mines. We knew you hadn't abandoned us, that you would never abandon us. We knew that one day you would come back. Now here you are, here in Mozambique once again. We just knew you would come, and you did."

By 1982 the first open signs of disillusionment with Marxism were beginning to surface. The tide was beginning to turn.

*   *   *

The governor of the province leaned back in his chair and paused, as if to choose his words carefully. "We, the government," he said, "made many mistakes back then." He did not say what those mistakes were; he didn't need to. He knew that we knew what they were: the persecution of the church in Mozambique, the imprisonment of our missionaries, the intimidation of believers, the propaganda against religion in general and Christianity in particular, all of this, and more. "But we are trying to rectify those mistakes," he emphasized. "We welcome the missionaries in Mozambique. We welcome the Church of the Nazarene in our country. We know its record. We know what it has done in this province. It has shown concern through the food shipments at this time of drought and great need. The people have confidence in it. They know the Nazarene missionaries, and trust them, and would like to see them back again. Yes, indeed, we made many mistakes back then. But all that is now in the past. Things have changed. We must move forward."

And move forward we did, because things had changed and were changing.

*   *   *

Promises. Promises. Promises. We were tired of them. They surfaced at regular intervals and were duly passed on to the Nazarene constituency. The Tavane Mission Station was to be denationalized, as well as the Mavengane District Center and certain local churches. But we had heard it all before.

Then the promises began to be fulfilled. Local church buildings were denationalized.

Rev. Simeon Mathe wrote:

> I would like to tell you an amazing thing that happened on our district. The Fujuca church has been returned to us! [Fujuca is a small village in a bush area of southern Mozambique.]
>
> The people had all been scattered abroad, so we had a special ceremony to reorganize the church. It had fallen into ruins. You would hardly have recognized it. It is no longer the church that you knew. You would weep if you saw it. Almost everything else in the village has been destroyed, except the church and the parsonage. But even these are in a sorrowful state. Doors and windows are missing.
>
> The community was sneering and laughing cynically at us as we tried to reorganize things and rededicate the church.
>
> The district superintendent read from Psalm 119, then from Psalm 136.
>
> The women of the Fujuca church sang with deep feeling and joy. They were so thankful to have their church back. Then District Superintendent Langa spoke, and said: "The Church of the Nazarene is now open." There were 176 people at the opening of the church. We were greatly blessed on that day.

Rev. Mathe, who was and is the pastor of the Tavane church, added a footnote: "I, the writer, continue to stay at what was the Tavane Nazarene Mission. I long for the day when the Tavane Mission will be returned to us. When we will reorganize and dedicate it, just as we have done with Fujuca. In Tavane, we hold our services under a tree. We cannot enter our church on the station. Please pray for us."

* * *

The Tavane Mission was one of the last mission properties to be handed back to the church in the rural areas.

"It was a great day," reported Carlota Langa, who is the coordinator of the children's work on the Mavengane

19

District. "That day in November 1990, the Tavane Mission Station was officially handed back to us. It was a great privilege to be one of those present." The church and some of the other buildings are still being used by the soldiers, because of the emergency situation. But, otherwise, the mission reclaimed its own on that day.

Part of the Tavane Mission Station as it is today

It was a "glory march." A great crowd of Nazarenes, singing and praising God, moved across the grounds. Into the tabernacle they marched, where, in days gone by, they had attended the annual camp meetings of the Manjacaze District. They read Psalm 95, which was so expressive of their confidence in God through the years. God, their Hope, their Rock, had brought them to this day.

> Come, let us sing for joy to the Lord;
> let us shout to the Rock of our salvation.
> Let us come before him with thanksgiving
> and extol him with music and song. . . .

Come, let us bow down in worship,
let us kneel before the Lord our Maker;
for he is our God and we are the people of his pasture,
the flock under his care.
vv. 1-2, 6-7

This was the day they had longed for and prayed for. It was the Day of Celebration, the day they rededicated the Tavane Mission to its sacred purpose, as an institution—as the "chief village"—of the Church of the Nazarene in the Gaza province.

A rural church that had been nationalized, now denationalized and returned to the Christians.

* * *

He was the government official who was assigned the task of returning to the Church of the Nazarene certain properties that had been confiscated by the authorities. He went with District Superintendent Langa to each of the properties in turn; to the Tavane Mission Station, to the Mavengane District Center, and to two local churches.

"I had done this same thing for other denominations,"

he said later. "But somehow this was not the same. The Nazarenes were different. They just impressed me somehow. Their church impressed me, too, as I went from place to place with Rev. Langa. I got to know the Nazarenes and became acquainted with their work and their ways of worship. I started to attend the local Church of the Nazarene where I lived. Then I got saved. And then I became a Nazarene."

*   *   *

There have been many ups and downs, many disappointments. The church is still suffering the consequences of that postindependence period. For various reasons, not all church properties have been returned. One thing is certain. The Marxist era has now drawn to a close and a new day has dawned.

▶▶ **2** ◀◀

"The Elephants, They Fight"

It dominates every conversation, casts its shadow over every home, strikes fear into every heart, and brings tragedy to every family. The rural areas of Mozambique have been devastated by it. All of life has been disrupted by it—the bush war.

It is an unfolding story of bloodshed and unbelievable human suffering, a brutal and savage war. *"Tiko ra hisa,"* say the Shangaans—which means, "The land, it is burning" (with the heat of war). It is a land without peace, where thousands upon thousands of people have fled from their homes. They have fled from the war zones and the groups of armed men who stalk the bush country, robbing, pillaging, terrorizing.

Johane explained:

> We Africans have a saying about elephants. Sometimes two elephants will quarrel with each other. They become aggressive. "The elephants, they fight." They are huge beasts, these elephants. They are locked in deadly battle. The sound of the battle can be heard throughout the bush.
>
> But who is it—what is it—that suffers most in this fight between the great ones of the animal kingdom? Is it not the grass that they trample beneath their feet? When the elephants get tired of fighting, they walk away. But what do they leave behind them, on the field of battle? The grass.

23

But now it is crushed and broken. "The elephants, they fight." But it is the grass that suffers most.

So, you see, that is the way it is with this war. It is a war between the great ones—the government and its armed forces, on one hand, and the rebel movement on the other. These two great elephants, they fight. But it is the ordinary people like me who suffer most. We are the grass beneath their feet, crushed and broken.

When is it all going to end? When is it all going to end? When, indeed . . . ?

* * *

In the bush country of southern Mozambique, the sun was beginning to set, the shadows to lengthen. The Shangaan people were beginning to snuff out the kerosene lamps in their little mud-and-thatch homes and to settle down for the night. Up on the hillside, the soldiers who occupied the Nazarene mission station were also preparing for nightfall by posting guards. They wanted to be sure that all possible security measures had been taken. After all, this was a war zone.

The attack, when it came, was sudden, without warning.

However, the soldiers on the mission were alert, and the attackers were beaten off. As they withdrew, the band of guerrillas took prisoners with them. The people they captured were those who lived beyond the perimeter of the mission. Most of the prisoners were Nazarenes. Among them was old Dia Mucavele. He was one of the church's early converts in Mozambique. Dia Mucavele's name will always be associated with the pioneering days of Nazarene missions in that country. Pioneer Mozambique missionaries like Mary Cooper influenced him. He was a layman, and yet a preacher. He was a builder by trade and a builder of churches by choice. But now in his old age, he was in the hands of terrorists—he and his wife, Marita, and his four grandchildren.

They were force-marched through the bush, at a pace

that old Marita could not maintain. She stumbled through the deep, sandy terrain, hardly able to drag one foot after the other. She fell. She picked herself up with the help of her husband. She waded across streams. She fell again and was roughly dragged to her feet by her captors. There was no more strength in her. She could not keep up with the others. She was a liability. So they shot her.

Who can describe the anguish that must have gripped the heart of old Dia at this time? He was forced to go on, leaving the body of his life's companion on the trail. Who can describe what her grandchildren must have felt?

Old Dia and his two grandsons were taken to the same rebel camp. The two granddaughters were taken to a different one. One day, his grandsons came to him and said that they were going to try to escape. They wanted him to go with them. But their grandfather was adamant: "You go, my children, and God be with you. But I must stay. I am old. I cannot walk fast. I cannot run. I would only hold you back. They would catch you because of me, and they would kill you. Yes, I know that you bring me water, and you help me to find food. But you must think of yourselves, not of me. You must go, but I must stay." So they went and managed to escape.

It was not long afterward that other escapees reported the death of Dia Mucavele. Old and weak as he was, he could no longer withstand the ravages of hunger and heartbreak.

A meeting of all the Mucavele family members was arranged to talk over the death of the old ones. Nelisha, one of Dia's daughters, was among those who traveled to the prearranged meeting place. She got a lift in a Land Rover. She sat at the back of the vehicle. Her baby was with a friend in the front. They bumped along the dirt roads, and everything seemed to be fine. Then they were ambushed by terrorists. The car skidded to a halt in the deep sand. Everybody fled into the bush, including Nelisha. Then she realized that the person who had her baby was not one of those who escaped. She stopped in her panic-stricken flight to safety, turned around, and deliberately went back to the car and to the group of armed men who surrounded it. They killed her baby in front of her eyes. Then they killed her.

Ironically, it was the terrorist who killed her who told the story of how she died, after he surrendered to the authorities as part of an armistice. He described the whole incident, in detail, in a public meeting.

* * *

"There was no time to bring anything else," said Eliza. There was a note of great sadness in her voice and a far-off look in her eyes, as if she were seeing something we could not see. She was reliving experiences we could not share. Behind those tragic eyes, we knew, she was seeing the home she had left behind her when she fled to the displaced persons camp at Mufa, in northern Mozambique. She was reliving the orderly life she had lived in that rural homestead, so many miles from where she now was. She was thinking of the domestic chores and the daily routine. She was seeing her children playing or working around the homestead, the gardens she had cultivated. The pots and pans, the familiar things she had handled and worked with in that domestic setting, her previous life, her meager possessions, everything, was gone.

And yet not everything. Not quite everything.

"When we heard the terrorists coming," she said, "we just had to leave everything behind and run for our lives. There was no time to think of what or how much I should take. It was just a matter of rounding up the children and getting away from there as quickly as possible. But there was one thing I had to take. My Bible. I couldn't leave that behind, could I? And, oh yes, I also took a little bag of flour to make porridge." She smiled for the first time, and stretched out her hand to show us the Bible, before lapsing back into her quiet, introspective mood.

26

Eliza, with her Bible

Eliza, the little unassuming lady who couldn't leave her Bible behind her, put it to good use at the Mufa refugee camp. She assumed the role of spiritual leader of the Nazarene group that started meeting there. She was a displaced pastor, ministering to a displaced people.

Eliza's church was situated on a small hill at the side of the camp. The church was built of reeds tied together with the bark of trees. We met together there in that church and enjoyed a time of fellowship and worship. Yet the most vivid memory of that time came at the end of the service. From the church on the hill we had a panoramic view of the whole camp. We watched as the people made their way down the hill. They began to sing, quietly at first, then with increasing vigor, enthusiasm, and joy. It was a deeply moving experience. We looked out across that sprawling camp laid out below us, with its arid and desolate landscape. We felt the shimmering heat. We saw that great congregation of people as they made their way back to their little reed shacks. They were displaced and homeless, yet still singing. Eliza was among them, with her Bible.

* * *

"They come across the river at night," explained my companion. "They steal or destroy whatever they want. Then they go back to the other side of the river before daylight."

Every five or six miles we passed through a little village on the main road—a dirt road—to the Limpopo Valley area of southern Mozambique. The villages consisted of a few straggling houses and a store or two. Almost every store had been gutted and burned. Further on, as we got nearer to our destination, the villages became fewer and fewer. We were now passing the mud-and-reed homesteads of the Limpopo people, on both sides of the road. The difference here was that most of the homesteads had, like the stores we had seen earlier on, been destroyed. Just the broken walls remained, if anything, little mounds of ash and debris. Stark. Pitiable. Desolate.

Is it ever going to end, this madness, this wanton destruction of property, this callous disregard for human life?

Soldier in a displaced persons camp, a reminder of the bush war beyond the camp's perimeter.

That was the question we asked each other as we continued on our way—the question we ask ourselves, and everyone else, all the time. Yet, strangely enough, we were soon to see this question in a new, more hopeful light, before we made the return trip on the same road.

We were to have an interview with the governor of the province, in the town of Chokwe. As a courtesy, the local administrator offered us accommodation in a house used by the administration for official visitors. On the morning we were to leave, we were asked not to delay too much, because they needed our rooms. A delegation was due in at any time from the rebel movement itself. Peace talks were in progress in a foreign country between the rebels and the government. There was no cease-fire, yet. This delegation had been dispatched to the Limpopo region under the terms of a partial agreement between the two parties.

We saw them as we left Chokwe, in an official-looking car, heading into the town. They were flying a little flag that we had never seen before, with uniforms that were also strange to us. They were on their way to the house we had just left, to the rooms we had just vacated. We looked at each other. There was silence. Each one was lost in his own thoughts. Was there, after all, some glimmer of hope, some prospect of peace for this war-torn country?

*   *   *

It was an awe-inspiring spectacle. Hundreds of people gathered together in a huge circle, outside Maputo Central Church. The Scripture was read, and a hushed silence settled over the great gathering. A sobbing cry broke out, and a young man detached himself from the crowd and staggered into the center of the circle. The pastor of the church supported him on one side, and the assistant pastor on the other. He was weak in body, anguished in soul, like someone about to engage in the supreme battle of his life.

Who was he? Let us ask, rather, "What has he been?" and "What is he about to become?"

He had been a demon worshiper. He had also been a member of a band of terrorists that spread death and destruction in the rural areas.

Now he was engaged in the most decisive battle of his life—against the demons that held sway in his inner being. He battled against the spiritual forces that fought savagely for the possession of his soul.

It was, indeed, an awesome spectacle to watch the spiritual drama enacted in the center of that great circle of Nazarenes. The demon things were gathered into a little pile—things that "belonged" to the demons, things that bound him to that dark world of the spirits. Destroy these, and he destroys the spirits' power over him. Let even one of these "demon things" remain in his possession, and those dark forces will still claim him as their own.

The battle was joined. The trembling hands of the young man took the match, struck it, and set the kerosene-soaked pile alight. He wept for joy and raised his hands in prayer and thanksgiving. Light had come into his darkness. From that great gathering of Nazarenes arose a song of triumph that echoed through the courts of heaven and caused the angels to rejoice. "Then I looked and heard the voice of many angels, numbering thousands upon thousands, and ten thousand times ten thousand. . . . Then I heard every creature in heaven and on earth and under the earth and on the sea, and all that is in them, singing: 'To him who sits on the throne and to the Lamb be praise and honor and glory and power, for ever and ever!'" (Rev. 5:11, 13).

My heart was stirred as I witnessed this powerful demonstration of God at work in a human life. Here was the answer, the final answer, for Mozambique and for its people. The answer is found in Christ, in a gospel that can change men and women. That gospel applies the balm of Gilead to the broken hearts and lives of people. People who live in a land of burning anger and raw, unrelenting anguish need suffer no more.

▶▶ 3 ◀◀

A Journey
into the Bush

"And the road? Any troubles on the Tavane road at the moment? Are things any better out there, or just the same?"

Benjamin Langa, superintendent of the Manjacaze District, smiled at my questions, and said: "On the whole, things are not too bad. It has been a while since we heard of any attacks. We'll keep our ears open and, all being well, we'll head for Tavane in a few days' time."

We were in Xai-Xai, Heather and I. It is the principal town of the Gaza province, more than 100 miles north of Maputo. Just a short distance to the east of us was the coast, and the Indian Ocean. Inland, to the west of us, stretched the bush country that is so typical of the Gaza province. It is a flat landscape of scattered bushes and trees, winding trails and dirt roads. Dotted here and there throughout the bushveld are the villages of the Shangaan people. Gaza. Birthplace of the Church of the Nazarene in Mozambique. Home of our Manjacaze, Mavengane, and Limpopo districts.

Some miles into that expanse of country, on a hill overlooking a valley, was the Tavane Mission Station.

* * *

It was good to be back in Gaza, even if it was only for a 10-day visit. It was good to be able to plan a trip out to

Tavane—or Machulane, as they call it these days. We just had to be careful, that's all. We monitored the situation in the countryside before leaving Xai-Xai. We checked with people who had just been traveling outside the town limits—bus drivers, truck drivers, anybody. We would just have to keep our ears open, as Benjamin said.

About two days before we left on our journey, we were at a truck stop on the main road leading out of town, with our ears open. We listened to an excited truck driver who had left Xai-Xai earlier in the day, heading northward. He was now back in Xai-Xai. "At the turnoff for Manjacaze," he said, gesticulating and speaking in a loud voice, for all to hear, "they killed some people, and gouged out the eyes of others! I saw it, I tell you. Believe me, I saw it!"

The Manjacaze turnoff was the road to Tavane, so we delayed our departure for another day. "The thing is," explained Benjamin, "this is a good time to go, because the terrorists know that an incident like this alerts the security forces to their presence. They have probably moved away to some other area."

We followed the main road (the only tarred road that went north) for a number of miles until we came to the Manjacaze turnoff. We then turned inland onto a dirt road and resigned ourselves to a rough ride as the pickup truck slid and slithered along at a good pace on its sandy surface.

"Just ahead of us, round the next bend," said Benjamin Langa, at one point, "is a trail that criss-crosses this road. It is known to be used a lot by the rebels. They cross the road just there, going north." We were all very quiet, then. Our eyes fixed on the bend ahead, wondering what lay beyond it. We soon found out. As we rounded the bend, we saw the trail that cut across the road. Two armed men in military garb were waving us down. Soldiers? Or terrorists? Would Benjamin stop? No. He wasn't stopping. He was just driving on. Then we were around another bend, and away.

"Do you think they were government soldiers?" I asked Rev. Langa, when the tension in the car had eased a bit. "Or terrorists?"

He shrugged. "I don't know," he said frankly. "I really don't know."

We did know that the next group of military men we saw were government soldiers. The only problem was that we did not see them in time. Or, at least, Benjamin did not see the cord stretched across the road as we came driving round yet another bend. On a tarred road, there would be no problem, even with the poor brakes that our pickup had. But a dirt road is quite a different story. With his foot hard on the brake, and our vehicle careening inexorably toward the roadblock, Benjamin still had the time, and the presence of mind, to warn us that, if we broke through the roadblock they would shoot out our tires. Hopefully, they would only shoot the tires. Our pace was beginning to slow and the pickup slid to a stop at the cord across the road, gently touching it, stretching it just a little.

One of the soldiers, grim-faced, came marching round to the driver's side of the vehicle. Then his face broke into a smile. "Oh," he said, "it's you, Rev. Langa!" It turned out that they knew each other. He brushed aside Benjamin's apologies and treated us with great courtesy. We continued on our way.

We soon reached the little town of Manjacaze. We had known this town well in happier times. Manjacaze is the administrative center for the whole area. Many people had been massacred here some three years before in a terrorist attack, and it had been attacked yet again in the last few months. We drove in silence around the few streets that made up this little community. This was no longer the Manjacaze that we had known. It was not even the Manjacaze that we had seen on our previous visit to this area, for half of the town had been destroyed.

On the outskirts of Manjacaze we stopped off at the Nazarene church, where we were met by a jubilant crowd

Some Manjacaze Nazarenes who welcomed us to their church outside the village.

of about 70 people. They escorted us into their little reed church, and we spent a short time of fellowship with them. I was reminded yet again how genuinely happy these Gaza Nazarenes are to have visitors. Especially in these days, and in this grim and violent environment, visitors are few and far between.

We bade our Manjacaze Christians farewell and set off on the second and final leg of our journey, past another military roadblock. We were on the winding dirt road that would take us to Tavane.

As we drove further away from Manjacaze, and further into the bush beyond, we saw fewer and fewer people. Then it seemed as if we entered a silent, almost uninhabited world. Only the sounds of the bush could be heard, and the belabored sound of the pickup truck as it pushed its way through the inhospitable terrain. The people had left the region, to find refuge in towns, villages, and populated areas where there was more security. Some were in Manjacaze, some in Xai-Xai, many in Maputo.

Those who were close by would slip back to their homes during the day and cultivate their gardens, then get out again before darkness fell.

There was a tightness in our stomachs as we drove wearily on. The surrounding bush seemed thicker than usual, more menacing. The silence became oppressive. Then familiar landmarks began to appear, and villages, Shangaan villages. We passed people along the road and called greetings to them. We were on the home stretch and then we were home in Tavane, the main station of the Church of the Nazarene in the Gaza province of Mozambique.

"We sleep with fear," said the Tavane pastor later, after we had been royally welcomed to the mission, and were relaxing over a meal of rice, *vuswa* (hard porridge), and chicken. "But we are really quite safe here. The station is ringed with mines. There is also a strong contingent of soldiers. We have been attacked about three times, but each time the attackers have been driven off. You can see the bullet holes in the walls of the church. The old mission office, as you know, has been badly damaged. One of the hospital buildings has had its roof blown off. It is when we

Arrival at the Tavane Mission Station

leave the station that we feel most vulnerable. On the road to Manjacaze is when we are really afraid."

* * *

This was not our first visit to Tavane. But it was the first time for us to have spent the night there since 1975. We spent it in a former missionary home, where our missionary nurses had lived, and where a government nurse and his family now live.

It was a strange night.

One of the things that always strikes you about Tavane is the sense of silence and solitude after darkness falls. The silence and the solitude of the African bush is an experience so utterly different from that of the city dweller. The stars are so bright, so vivid. They shine down in lonely splendor upon a great expanse of bush country, far from the competing lights of the urban areas. Among those twinkling lights in God's heaven is that unique constellation of stars arranged in the form of a cross—the Southern Cross. It looks down upon a troubled country, upon a brave and suffering people, a people who sleep with fear. It reminds them of a hill far away, of an old rugged Cross, and of a Savior who understands their sufferings and wants to share their burdens.

These thoughts were running through my mind that night as we settled down to sleep. It was dark. There was no noise, except the soothing sounds of the bush. Then we heard the voice; a strange, solitary voice from somewhere on the mission station. That voice, somehow accentuated by the background of silence, sent chills down our spines. It called out into the darkness. Then an answering call came from the other side of the mission. Sentries on guard duty, they told us later, were keeping themselves awake and alert. They wanted to let the enemy know that they were ready for him. They called out into the surrounding bush, into the darkness where the terrorists might be lurking.

36

We finally fell asleep, with the voices still calling outside. The Southern Cross was holding its own sentinel in the somber night.

*   *   *

The next day, the Lord's Day, we made our way to the place of our morning service. It would not be in the church building, which was still used as a dormitory for the soldiers, but in a school hall on the other side of the mission.

The hall rapidly filled to overflowing with people. As I looked out across that great congregation, my heart was deeply stirred within me. Some of these people were from the mission itself, and others were from the surrounding areas. They had walked many miles to get here. Many of them I knew well, others were new to me. There was old Mamana Ana, a charter member who joined the Church of the Nazarene when it first came to this country and established itself in this area. There were many others, including preachers. We felt the presence of the Lord in our midst. The congregation sang the songs of Zion as only a Shangaan congregation can sing. When I stood to preach, I was conscious of the fact that I was the first missionary to have a service in Tavane since 1975. "Heaven came down, and glory filled our souls" as we worshiped the Lord together.

With the morning service over, we all gathered in the tabernacle—the open auditorium where camp meetings are held—for the closing exercises of the *Mintlawa* program. (*Mintlawa* is a children's and youth program that is unique to Mozambique, even though, for statistical purposes, it is given the name of "Caravans," an established Nazarene ministry to children.) It is one of the church's most effective means of outreach to children and young people in Mozambique. It is a ministry that involves the use of traveling teacher-trainers who teach such things as sewing, knitting, hygiene, and etiquette in various centers scattered throughout the districts. But, above all, it is a spiritual ministry, a Bible-teaching ministry that has been remarkably successful in reaching into non-Christian homes and winning the children and young people for Christ.

There in Tavane, in the tabernacle, the *Mintlawa* children showed us the things they had made, sang for us, and some of them received prizes. At the beginning of the Marxist period, the *Mintlawa* program had been frowned on by the authorities. In fact, it had been discontinued, except in some areas where the teachers bravely and tirelessly carried on the work. Now, as I looked at those scores of children and young people, and saw the sterling work done by those who ministered among them, my heart was stirred. The church was in good hands today, and it would be in good hands tomorrow.

* * *

It was time to head back to Xai-Xai. A great crowd of people saw us off, singing and waving as we drove off. At the back of the truck we had a number of *Mintlawa* teachers. We also had a soldier who had been wounded in a skirmish with terrorists during the night.

The return journey proved to be a less somber affair than the trip out to the mission the day before—thanks to our folk at the back of the truck. After we left the wounded soldier off at the Manjacaze hospital, and headed for home, they began to sing. They sang with great zest and enthusiasm, uninhibited and free. People on the road stopped to stare and listen. Their singing would have carried far and wide in the bush country in which we were traveling. Hymn after hymn they sang. Especially that old Shangaan favorite *"Yi Fikile Evangeli"*—"The Gospel Has Arrived." It is a hymn they always sing at the opening of a new church, and on all special occasions; a hymn that reminds them of when the gospel first came to Gaza and of the light that flooded into their darkness. They sing of the Word that was preached throughout the land of Gaza and of the joy that now fills their hearts as they think of that glorious message that came to their land:

Swoswi hi li: Aleluya,
Yi fikile Evangeli!

And now we can say: Hallelujah,
The gospel has arrived!

They were still singing when we arrived in Xai-Xai.

▶▶ **4** ◀◀

The *Deslocados* and the *Refugiados*

Thousands upon thousands of them—whole populations of people have been uprooted from their homes. They are the displaced persons, the *deslocados*, displaced because of the years of drought. When nothing would grow, the peasant farmers of Mozambique would leave their homes and *maxambas* (gardens), with their dead and dying crops. They would trek to the villages, towns, and cities to find food and clothing for themselves and for their families.

Then came the years of war, to heap further misery upon a people already devastated by the years of drought and famine. It created yet another generation of *deslocados* to add to the million or more who were now unable to return home because of the security situation. What was the alternative to fleeing from your home? The alternative was to be alert at all times, your adrenalin at a constant high. It meant hiding your possessions and money in holes in the ground, or sleeping in the bushes at night rather than in your own bed. It meant living in daily—and nightly—fear of abduction, torture, and death. That was the alternative, and still is.

It is the way that many people have chosen to live in the bush areas of Mozambique. They prefer a harsh and dangerous existence in their own homes, rather than the precarious life of the *deslocado* in the urban areas.

Precarious certainly describes the life of the displaced person, trying to eke out a living in the villages, towns, and cities of Mozambique or in the displaced persons camps. It is a dependent life, dependent on the charity of others. There is little or no employment. Precarious, yes, but safe, at least relatively so. What more can you ask?

Then there are the *refugiados*—the refugees. People who not only abandon their homes and flee to places of safety within Mozambique but also cross national borders to escape the grinding poverty and misery of their lives. They find refuge in the neighboring countries of Swaziland, South Africa, Zimbabwe, Zambia, Malawi, and Tanzania. They usually flee from their homes at night, and in small groups. They walk many, many miles, passing through highly dangerous areas. They cross national borders that are often mined. When they arrive at their destination, they are malnourished and ill, if, in fact, they arrive at all.

Displaced persons. Refugees. Does it really matter what we call them? They are the homeless, the dispossessed, the poor, the downtrodden—the Mozambicans.

* * *

We set out in our four-wheel drive vehicle to visit the displaced persons camps in the Tete province of northern Mozambique. As we drove out of the town of Tete onto the bridge that spans the broad Zambezi River, we saw people bathing and washing clothes in the crocodile-infested waters. Then we were off the bridge and into the bush country on the other side.

There had been no rain in this part of Mozambique for a very long time. It was extremely hot. The sun shone relentlessly from a cloudless sky. Everything was dry, arid, desertlike. We left clouds of fine, dry dust behind us as we bumped along the winding dirt road.

We passed poverty-stricken African homesteads on the way. Here and there we saw people working in their

41

Young boys in a displaced persons camp in the Tete area

maxambas, scratching in the hard, dusty earth. They were trying to coax some corn or vegetables, any kind of plant life, from its gray, unyielding surface. Gnarled, dead trees were a dominant feature of the arid landscape. Then there were the goats, everlastingly stretching out their necks to find some remaining green leaves on the higher branches of the shrub trees.

Yet, not so very far away was the great Zambezi River. Those who lived by the riverside, and were fortunate enough to have a water pump, could draw water from that huge river to irrigate their *maxambas*. But for the vast majority of people that was only a dream. Perhaps, in the future, some basic infrastructure will be set up in this desolate region. Then, perhaps—as in the prophetic vision—the desert and the parched land will be transformed. The wilderness will rejoice and blossom like the rose. The desert will burst into bloom. Water will gush forth in the wilderness, and there will be streams in the desert. The burning sand will become a pool. In the haunts where jackals once lay, grass will grow. And in the *maxambas* of the people, there will be corn and rice and vegetables . . . but not yet. Someday, perhaps, this scorched earth will produce in abundance. But today is still today. And the wilderness still holds sway in this part of Africa.

After about a two-hour journey, we drove into the Padwe displaced persons camp. The camp is composed of hundreds of little reed huts, big enough for one or two people to lie down in, but not to stand up in. The huts are used only for sleeping. The camp accommodates over 2,000 people, many of whom were there to welcome us to their desolate domain. They were people in rags, hungry people. The children had distended abdomens and reddish hair—the classic signs of malnutrition. Some were listlessly kicking around a ball made of plastic bags. The camp was full of men unable to support their families, women unable to feed their babies. They were people completely dependent on the charity of others for their very survival.

Displaced Mozambicans and their sleeping huts in the camps

"Why do we do it?" I asked them later, standing in the shade of a tree at a rough table, with hundreds of people sitting on the ground all around me. "Why do we go to all the expense of sending containers of food and clothing into Mozambique? Why do we take the time to do all this, to work so hard in the service of others? Why do our Nazarenes overseas send you the clothes that you wear, the food that you eat, the soap with which you wash yourself, the seed that you sow in your gardens? Why? It is not because we are a humanitarian agency, a relief agency, a government agency, a United Nations agency. Why, then? It is because we are compelled by the love of Christ. We love you because of Him. We care for you because of Him. What we give you, we give you in His name. Do not thank us. Thank God."

Then it was on to the Benga camp, with its 6,000 *deslocados* crowded into reed huts and hundreds of tents supplied by a UN relief agency. We went to other places, too, but the scenario was always the same: homeless people, poorly clothed and poorly fed, utterly destitute of all the basic things of life that most of us take for granted.

* * *

"They were beginning to fight for the used clothing," said Rev. Matias Beta, superintendent of the Tete District, waving his arms in a gesture of helplessness. "They were actually getting themselves worked up so much that they were ready to fight each other for it."

Nazarenes from overseas had sent containers filled with used clothing and other relief goods. Most of these goods were distributed in the displaced persons camps in the Tete province.

When one of the first trucks arrived at Benga, the camp authorities already had a list of all the families in the camp, with their names, and the number of children in each family. It was all well organized, as it always is. Everybody would get something, no matter how little.

Every family would be given a certain amount of clothing, in accordance with the number of people in the family.

They were all lined up in families. The name of a certain family was called, and the members of that family came up to receive their portion. Then another family came. And another. And another. But the people further away from the point of distribution began to get restless. They saw the pile of clothing getting smaller. They thought there was not going to be anything left for them, so they began to move forward, pushing, shoving, shouting. They were arguing with each other, and an ugly situation was developing. Everything was threatening to dissolve into chaos.

"It was really bad," said Rev. Beta. "Then the authorities stopped the distribution altogether. They told the people that other Nazarene containers would be arriving from time to time. Those who did not receive anything this time would receive it later. Their turn would certainly come. There would be enough for everybody. Everybody would get their share. They told them that nothing more would be given out until everybody settled down and waited until their names were called. The people were somewhat satisfied by this, and the distribution was finally completed without any further problems.

"You see," he added, rather apologetically, appealing for my understanding, "they have so very little. So they feel terribly upset when they think they are going to be turned away empty-handed."

As it happened, they were not turned away empty-handed. More containers arrived from Nazarenes overseas. Everybody received something, however little.

Nor was that the end of the emergency relief effort. As the church overseas began to hear about the plight of the people in the Tete region of Mozambique, further relief efforts were made to do something about it. Through Nazarene Compassionate Ministries, shipments of maize (corn) were sent to Tete, for distribution through the Church of the Nazarene. Most of this went to the displaced persons camps and was distributed over a wide area, using transport provided by the provincial authorities.

"Now we are real people again," wrote one of our Tete Nazarenes, in a letter of thanks. "Before, we were hungry and naked, and nobody seemed to care. Then you, our beloved Nazarenes overseas, showed that you loved us— loved us enough to send clothes to cover our nakedness, and food to satisfy our hunger. We were no longer animals, something less than human. We have become real people again."

* * *

They all had a story about the flight from their homes. We heard many stories from many sources. Most of them walked many miles through the bush of the Mozambique side, leaving their homeland and entering South African territory. Their journey was through the Kruger National Park, with its trackless bush and wild animals. A terrible weariness and exhaustion gripped them all. They experienced painful blisters on their feet, intense heat, terrifying thirst, and the constant fear of being caught by the South African security forces and being sent back to Mozambique.

Two stories, however, caused us acute distress.

"Some people who just arrived today," they told us, "had a bad experience in the Skukuza area of the game reserve. One of the women in the group died. The men went off to find water. They found some and brought it back to the two remaining women. The men had to go off again to find more water, but when they came back the women were no longer there. They had disappeared. They couldn't find them anywhere."

Had they been taken by wild animals? Or wandered off and been lost? Had they been found by game rangers and taken somewhere? No one knew the answer to these questions. They just shrugged fatalistically and said, "Who knows? They just disappeared."

We then spoke to others, including the nurse in charge of the local clinic, to find out about another group who had arrived in the camp within the last few days. There were 13 of them, they told us. Thirteen people who managed to get as far as the game reserve. Ten of them died, and only 3 reached the refugee camp in South Africa. Only 3.

"How did they die?"

"It is the heat," they explained, "and the thirst. They just couldn't take it any longer." Again, that fatalistic shrug.

Where did they die? In the Skukuza area, they said.

Skukuza. From where we, ourselves, had just come. It is an area well-known for its wildlife: giraffe, warthog, elephant, hippo, lion, buffalo, and many kinds of buck. We had spent two very pleasant nights in a camp for visitors to the reserve, and two very pleasant days exploring the surrounding bush in our car.

It was just about that same time that 10 Mozambican refugees died. At that same time, 2 Mozambican women disappeared in the Skukuza bush. While we were viewing game and admiring a pride of lions, people had died.

On the "road of the lions" at Skukuza

The refugee camps are all situated close to the Kruger National Park because the Mozambican refugees' point of entry into South Africa is through the game reserve. On foot, it is a hazardous and dangerous journey.

"Are they still coming across?" I asked a group of refugees who had been in one of the camps for quite some time. With everybody clamoring to answer our questions, we were left in no doubt that Mozambicans were still leaving the Gaza province of southern Mozambique and entering South Africa as refugees.

▶▶ 5 ◀◀

"I Will Build
My Church"

It happened a long time ago, when the Church was young, alive, and vigorous. It confronted many difficulties. It fought for its very survival. Its members were scattered abroad. In the history book that relates the story of those days—the Acts of the Apostles—we are told: "Those who had been scattered preached the word wherever they went" (8:4).

That is the story of the Church, not only in Palestine, but in Mozambique; the story not only of the infant Church in those early days but of the Mozambique church in these modern times.

Picture the scene, the Mozambique scene. A country is reeling from the effects of drought, famine, and war. About a million Mozambicans are refugees in neighboring countries. Anywhere from 2 to 3 million displaced persons are within the country itself. People have been uprooted from their homes. Villages are abandoned. Other villages, new villages, in more secure areas, are springing up to accommodate the *deslocados*, the displaced people. Established villages have vastly increased populations. Towns and cities are trying desperately to deal with the influx of people from the outlying areas. People move in with family and friends in these urban areas or are allocated pieces of ground on which to erect makeshift dwellings.

Among these displaced people are Christians. Christians who, after being scattered abroad in this way, have preached the Word wherever they have gone.

It is an impressive record of Christian witness; of Christians who left their homes and their local churches behind them, but not their commitment to Christ. Believers are rubbing shoulders with unbelievers who may never have heard the gospel in their home areas but who are now hearing it—from their new neighbors.

Displaced Nazarenes have often found themselves far from their home churches. They have ended up in towns, villages, and displaced persons camps where there may or may not be other Nazarenes. If there is a Nazarene church there, they will attend it. If not, they will start one. They are witnesses, spreading the Word of God, extending the witness of the church. And the result? New preaching points. New churches. New converts. There is a Nazarene witness in areas of Mozambique where, before, the Church of the Nazarene was unknown or where the message of holiness had not yet reached.

It is the "yeast of the gospel." Working through the whole batch of dough. It spreads the influence of the Christian gospel throughout the country.

* * *

It is a large region in the Gaza province, through which the Limpopo River flows. It is bush country, well-populated. People work in their fields, cultivating. They support themselves and their families by the work of their own hands. Typical African homesteads serve their basic needs. It's not an idyllic situation, nor a romantic one, but just a normal Mozambique community, in a normal Mozambique setting. It is a functioning, integrated society, going about its business as it has done for centuries.

Then came the years of famine. Then came the war; then the trek away from the area. Homes were abandoned.

Cultivated fields were lying derelict and unproductive. Bush trails, defined over the years by the tramp of many feet, are now overgrown with weeds.

The churches were empty, abandoned, silent.

"It really is an interesting story," says Rev. Elias Mucasse, superintendent of the Limpopo District. "Twenty-five of our Limpopo District churches are no longer functioning on their old location. And we have no news of 6 other churches, no contact with them, because they are in bad war zones. We have only 14 churches that are operating normally, in their normal location."

Fourteen churches, out of a total of 45 on the district. And the other churches, the ones that were abandoned?

"They survived," says Rev. Mucasse firmly. There is a note of pride in his voice, and an undertone of wonder that adds weight to his words. "And that is the interesting part of the story. Of course, some of the people simply worshiped with other Nazarene congregations, if there was a Nazarene church in the area where they settled. But that was not always the case.

"Many times, the pastor would be the first to leave the old area. He would head for the Limpopo River and look for a sizable piece of ground; a place where there was security, and land for cultivation. He would organize things with the local authorities. Then he would send word to his people that there was a place for them."

Each Nazarene congregation, each Nazarene community, followed its pastor to the Limpopo valley and settled in the same area as its pastor. The congregation stayed together as a unit and reestablished the church in the new location. It was called by the same name it had at its original location. And why not? What did it matter if the name was a geographical one and was inappropriate for the new location? It was a symbol, an expression of faith, an affirmation that the church did not die at the old location. It lives on here by the side of the Limpopo River. One day it will be born anew, out there in the bush country.

* * *

The area of Boane is situated some miles west of the capital city of Maputo. Two things helped the fledgling little mission church there to establish itself in the community.

First, there was the strong woman of Boane. One day, Maputo District Superintendent Manuel Tshambe and his wife, Bessie, went to visit the church. "I preached," said Rev. Tshambe, "and then I made an altar call at the end. Among those who came to the altar was this woman. She was a drunkard. She brewed her own drink, and also sold it to others. She was also incredibly strong. Anyone in the community will tell you about that. Her strength is legendary. They will tell you that nobody could control her when she was drunk. She could lift six men at a time, three on each arm—such was her strength."

She got saved that day, at the altar, and has never touched an alcoholic drink since. She is now a faithful and active Nazarene and has a great testimony in the Boane community.

Then there was the wedding. A young couple fell in love and were married in the church. That was what impressed everyone, the fact that they got married. It was the first wedding in the Boane church. But it was more than that. "Common law" marriages were the order of the day in that part of the country. It was very rare for anyone to have a legally recognized wedding, to say nothing of a church wedding. So this first Nazarene wedding caused quite a stir. The officials in the registry office were very impressed by it and talked about it at great length. The other church denominations in Boane were equally impressed. Especially by the fact that it was a church pastored by a woman that had initiated the first wedding in the area.

The wedding not only has strengthened the Boane church but also has opened doors for the Church of the Nazarene in the area where the bride comes from—Antigos Combatentes, some two hours' walk from the church. The district already had plans to start work in that area. The local authorities there were so impressed by the Nazarene wedding in Boane that they readily approved the church's request for a building site in Antigos Combatentes. So the Boane church will soon have its first branch church.

And who was the lady pastor who arranged that first wedding in Boane? Mrs. Bessie Tshambe, wife of the Maputo District Superintendent. She felt constrained to offer herself as pastor of that little flock the Sunday after she witnessed the conversion of the strong woman of Boane. Bessie recently became the first woman to be ordained by the Church of the Nazarene in Mozambique. She now pastors the Maputo Central Church, in the capital.

* * *

Maputo. The Mozambican capital, a bustling metropolis, full of life, movement, and noise, used to be a tourist's paradise, with its fine beaches and semitropical climate. The city now struggles to resolve its enormous economic and social problems. Some of the old glamour remains, but that has been eclipsed by the new reality of poverty and overcrowding. The *deslocados* have replaced the *turistas* as a major feature of the city's life. Great numbers of them are concentrated around the edges of the city, occupying all the available open spaces within the city itself. Their pathetic little dwellings are now part of the landscape, a sad and tragic landscape.

This overcrowded city of some 2 million people is the heartland of the Maputo District of the Church of the Nazarene. It is the most developed and viable of all the Mozambique districts.

"It's so exciting to be there, on the Maputo District," commented one visitor, echoing similar words that have been spoken again and again by many others. "There is such a sense of movement, of things happening, of people being saved. The churches are so alive, so vigorous. Their witness is so spontaneous, and so effective. It's not surprising that they're just bursting at the seams with people."

* * *

Excitement. That's it. That's the feeling you get when you visit Maputo Central Church; the largest Nazarene church in Mozambique, and one of the largest churches in Nazarene Africa. Its growth, as one of our Mozambicans expressed it, is "a great wonder." And now it has a beautiful new sanctuary, only recently completed, thanks to a generous donation from a Nazarene family in California, to the financial assistance of the Africa regional office, and to Rev. Dennis Riggs for his tireless labor and building skills.

The preacher has just finished his message. It is a special meeting in Central Church, and people from other churches on the district are among those attending. From my vantage point on the platform I have a panoramic view of the great congregation spread out before me—more than 2,000 of them. I watch them as they sing. My heart is thrilled at the sight of almost 100 people at the altar, weeping, praying, seeking God. Others are still coming, making their way down the aisles, responding to the stirring message that we have just heard.

But will the local church ever be able to fill this huge new sanctuary, quite apart from district and other special meetings? That is the challenge that confronts it. That is the challenge that it has accepted.

Just come outside for a moment, onto the church grounds, where we will be able to see how this local church has dealt with such challenges before. We will view its history, as it were. View its history? Yes, view it, in three stages. Over there is the "old church," a rather run-down, corrugated iron structure that is still in use. It was the first church building on the present site. It holds about 500 people. Over there is the second church that was built when the first one became too small to accommodate the congre-

Part of the congregation in the new sanctuary at Maputo Central Church.

gation. It is still in use, of course—very much so. It holds about 1,000 people. And now we have this third church, because the second one was becoming too small for its growing congregation.

Yes, Central Church will be able to fill its new sanctuary. It has done it before. It can do it again.

* * *

"I ask myself," said one of the Maputo pastors, "'How has the church grown here in Maputo? How has it spread out? And how has all this come about?' We should think about these questions. We should ponder them."

We should indeed. And when we do ponder them, we find that much of the growth has come about through mother churches giving birth to daughter churches. Daughter churches then go on to start their own families.

Consider the family history of just three churches: Maputo Central Church, the Mavalane Church, and the Infulene Church. The one thing that is common to all three of these is that they have what they call *zonas*. House meetings, cottage meetings, branch Sunday Schools, call them what you will, they are extensions of the mother church, a network of them. Weeknight meetings are held in different zones or areas. Every area that has a few Nazarenes—or even one Nazarene willing to offer his house for the purpose—is a potential *zona*. A *zona* could develop into an organized church.

Central Church—the first church on the district, and the first Nazarene congregation in the capital—has always had a big heart as well as a big congregation. Ever willing to give its own members as founding members of a new church, Central Church has been responsible for starting no fewer than 10 churches, 2 of which are Mavalane and Infulene. "Like mother, like daughter," Mavalane has been responsible for starting 5 churches, including a branch church with 187 members that meets on the new Bible college property—the future College Church. The Infulene Church can take credit for 6. So there are 21 churches in all that came from 3.

A "daughter church" in a Maputo suburb

Yet it isn't always as simple as that. Not every mother church can claim, or does claim, to be totally responsible for having started a new church. Often, it is a joint effort. One church supplies some members, another sends a local preacher to take charge of the group, and so on. No set pattern. No rigid rules. It is frequently a matter of one church doing the planting, another doing the watering, and God giving the increase.

* * *

"We started another preaching point in Masinwane last year," explained Rev. Elifaz Mazimba, pastor of the Infulene Church. "We hope that one of our members who lives in that area will take charge of it and also take some studies at the Extension Bible School. Or maybe one of the current Bible school students could take it over. I'm sure they would be delighted to be given the opportunity to study and, at the same time, to put their study into practice in Masinwane. Don't you agree?"

I agreed. Definitely.

"There is nothing else," he added, "that's more important than extending the work of the church. At least, that's the way we do things here, in our congregation. That's how we grow."

How did the mother church know when its daughter church was ready to be turned over to the district? To what degree would it be able to support itself at that point?

"Well," responded Elifaz, in a voice that clearly indicated that I had asked the right question, "we want a daughter church to grow in everything. Spiritually, yes. Which is why we are now studying the spiritual growth of the members at Masinwane. But also financially, and we are trying to see how the 20 or so people there—mostly women—could support a pastor. They must also learn to pay their district budget, and other budgets."

Elifaz paused, grinned that infectious grin of his, and concluded by saying, "We don't want them to be a burden to the district, do we? The district is burdened enough with expenses of its own. Nor do we want our daughter church to be a burden to the general church, because that would mean that our daughter had not yet grown up, not yet reached adulthood. Isn't that right?"

Once again, I agreed. How could I do otherwise?

"If our daughter church is a burden, like I have just said, she is still only a child, who gives work to her father. We must do everything possible, today, to bring our daughter church to maturity, so that it won't be a burden for its father tomorrow! Right?"

Right.

* * *

The date is October 1992. It is a historic date for the Maputo District, and for the Church of the Nazarene in Mozambique. It is the occasion of the Maputo District Assembly. General Superintendent Raymond W. Hurn chairs the last assembly of the district as a mission district. This is the assembly in which this work of God in the nation's capital becomes a regular district of the Church of the Nazarene, under the leadership of District Superintendent Manuel Tshambe. It is the first of the Mozambique districts to attain regular status. Congratulations, Maputo. We salute you.

During this assembly another drama unfolds that is of historic importance, not only for the church, but for the entire Mozambique nation. This drama is being played out thousands of miles away in Rome. The ceasefire negotiations have been finalized between the Mozambique National Resistance and the Mozambique government. The documents have been prepared, ready for signing. But one of the key players does not turn up for the signing. Stalemate ensues.

Back in Mozambique, the people nervously await the final outcome. They are torn between hope and fear. Corporately we pray that it will all come together—that the signing will take place and that the savage bush war will be brought to an end.

It is in the middle of one of the assembly sessions. It is business as usual. Then there is a stir among the delegates. Someone has just slipped in with the news: *a ceasefire has been signed.* There is a spontaneous burst of praise. We stand. We sing. We weep. It is an awesome and moving spectacle.

As it happened, the actual signing did not take place until the next day, October 4, after the tears and the praises of the Mozambique people had already been seen and heard in heaven.

There is still a long and difficult road ahead, with national elections scheduled for the latter part of 1993. But hopes are high. Hopes of peace after years of war.

▶▶ 6 ◀◀

The Call
of the North

"It is your decision," I told him. "Yours alone. I can't make it for you. But we must know. We must be able to plan. Everything else is in place. The rest is up to you."

Would Jonas be willing to go North?

The North, or rather the Northeast, to be more exact, has central Mozambique thrown in for good measure. But from where we stood, in the capital city of Maputo, in the southern part of the country, it was the North.

At this time, most Nazarene work in Mozambique was confined to the southern regions of the country. We were well established in the South. We had developed sound national leadership and were experiencing good church growth there. It was the core of Nazarene work in the country, where the heart of the church beat strongest.

And yet, always there was the call of the North. Persistent. Persuasive. Imperative. It was not something that we talked about a lot, not something that was vocalized in committees or that was the subject of debate. But it was there all the same, always there, a whispering challenge in the heart, a sense of urgency in the soul. It was a concern for fields north of us that were "ripe already unto harvest." It was time to break new ground, to look beyond the borders of the established districts. We needed to look to one of the most unevangelized parts of Africa.

* * *

It was still there, this call to go northward. It beckoned us on, urged us to step out in faith, to possess the land that the Lord our God had commanded us to possess. Could we do it? Would we do it? More to the point, could Jonas do it? Would he do it?

Jonas looked uncomfortable, shuffled his feet, and looked anywhere but at me. My heart sank. Were we about to experience another setback, another delay in implementing our dream of winning those northern peoples for Christ?

When doors started opening in the central and northern regions of Mozambique, Rev. Jonas Mulate was the one sent there on evangelistic and exploratory tours, beginning in 1984. Money was scarce, but the Mozambique Mission Council financed his trips from special funds. He would fly to the north and travel extensively in the central and northern provinces of Sofala, Manica, Nampula, Zambezia, Niassa, and Cabo Delgado. "There were no Nazarene churches in those areas," he reported, "and many have died without ever knowing about the Lord Jesus Christ. But God has blessed us since that visit. Preaching points have been established. The fire has spread to three of those provinces."

It was evident that the time was ripe for the Church of the Nazarene to raise the banner of holiness in those pioneer areas. A leader was needed for the work—a resident, pioneer pastor. We needed someone who had the potential to be a district superintendent as the work developed. Who better than Jonas Mulate?

Rev. Jonas Mulate was the pastor of the Maputo City Church at the time. The church had grown under his ministry to a membership of about 600. He was a born church planter, with a friendly, outgoing personality and a gift for personal witnessing. He was a soul winner, zealous for the Lord, eager to serve Him. Yes, Jonas was our man for the north.

So we asked him, and that is when the struggle began in his soul. He was greatly burdened for those pioneer areas, so he agreed to go. But the Lord was blessing his ministry in Maputo. His congregation pleaded with him to stay, saying that his work there was not yet finished. He had a wife and a large family to consider, so he backed off from his decision to go north. We approached him at a later date, with the same result.

But God was dealing with him, even as he stood before me, embarrassed and uncomfortable, as I waited for his response. Would he—this time—decide to go north?

No. Not this time. Not to the northern areas of Mozambique, but he was going to the midland counties of England. Jonas had always wanted to learn English. It was a lifelong ambition. Now, he explained, he had been offered a grant by the Christian Council of Mozambique to go to study English in the British Isles. It was an opportunity not to be missed. "When I come back from England," he assured me, "I will be ready to go to evangelize in central and northeastern Mozambique."

And that is just what he did, because God had called him.

"My church was doing well," he recalled later. "The Maputo City Church was a small church when I went there, but we soon received 11 new members. The blessing of the Lord continued upon us, until we had a membership of 120. The church still continued to grow until we had 350 full members.

"But we must fulfill the Great Commission of the Master. And to do that we must go to the north of Mozambique, where the message of full salvation has not yet been preached. 'I am ready . . . ,' as Paul said in Rom. 1:15. Ready to preach the Good News in the North. Long years have passed, and men are still living in the sea of sin. They cry out for help, but there is no one to comfort them. The people of northern Mozambique are in the grip of Satan, in the teeth of the lion. They need someone to free them from it. Our church has been in this country for many, many years. It is now 1988—yet the people of the North are still isolated, still waiting for us to go to them with the Good News.

"Months before, in 1987, the Lord opened the door for me to go up to those northern areas, to preach and to do exploratory evangelism. Many were converted. But the need is still so great, and I still get letters from up there, from people in those provinces, saying that they need physical and spiritual help. The Lord spoke to Moses in Deut. 2:3. He said, 'You have made your way around this hill country long enough; now turn north.' That is what we must do now. We have been around this southern part of our country long enough. The time has come for us to move out, to go north, to offer to others the message of holiness."

In 1989 we presented a proposal to our regional director, Dr. Richard Zanner, that central and northeastern Mozambique be declared pioneer areas, and that financial assistance be given for their development. The request was granted. In February 1990 Jonas went to Nampula to make arrangements for moving his family and belongings to that northern city. Soon, everything was in place, and his family was able to join him.

The move to the North had begun.

*   *   *

The city of Nampula is called the "Capital of the North." It is the third largest city in Mozambique and the most strategic location for our thrust into the northeastern areas of the country.

It all started before Jonas' move with Nazarenes from the South who came to work in Nampula. They started Nazarene meetings in the city, under the leadership of Julio Langa, originally a member of Maputo City Church. They contacted Jonas Mulate and appealed for his help in this fledgling work in the North. Jonas responded to the appeal and came for a seven-day visit. He found a congregation of about 50, meeting in Julio Langa's home. Ten people were converted during his visit. He also found that the group had been granted a prime plot of ground on which to build a church. This, in itself, was a miracle. Later, the house became too small, and they moved to a rented hall in the city. Construction of a new church was begun.

The Nampula Church is a healthy and dynamic church. It is the first Nazarene church in the vast northeastern area of Mozambique. It is alive and well in the "Capital of the North." The beginning was small, to be sure. It was but a candle, a burning candle that had been lit in the city of Nampula. That candle was destined to become a spreading flame of holiness evangelism with a flame that would reach into the other cities and provinces of the North.

* * *

The suburbs of Nampula began to feel the impact of the new Nazarene presence in the city. Jonas held revivals and witnessed for Christ everywhere he went. A witch doctor named Antonio was converted. For 30 years Antonio had worshiped the spirits of his ancestors. People would come to his village to seek his help. He would meet with them under the sacred tree where he practiced his divinatory rites. He would throw the sacred bones and divine the cause of the disease or other problem. Maybe it was caused by an ancestral spirit, or a witch, or by the patient having transgressed some taboo or other. The bones would reveal it all under the sacred tree. But, by the grace of God, the bones' days were numbered. On the very day that Antonio found Christ he enlisted the help of the Nazarenes to cut down his sacred tree. It was then burnt, along with the bones and other witch doctor's paraphernalia. The citadels of Satan were being breached by the power of the gospel of Christ.

Today, we have nine churches in the Nampula area alone, and the work is still growing.

The six Mozambique district superintendents. From left: Mario Matsinhe, Matias Beta, Elias Mucasse, Benjamin Langa, Jonas Mulate, and Manuel Tshambe.

"On one day alone," says Jonas, "many people were brought under the sound of the gospel on the train. I was on my way to the port town of Nacala. I distributed tracts on the train and shared the Portuguese-language *Herald of Holiness* with them. Many of them showed a great interest in the Church of the Nazarene and promised to look up the Nazarene group or church in their home areas. On this particular day, six girls, two boys, and seven women accepted Jesus Christ as their Savior. There was a woman on the train who came to me and told me that she had had a fight with her husband, and that she was going to commit suicide. The gospel reached her when she needed it most. She returned to her husband. We are hoping and praying that they will both become members of our church. We have now had six weddings."

* * *

The town of Lichinga is in the Niassa province, on the

65

eastern side of Lake Nyasa. It is close to the Malawi border but far from the Mozambique coast and from Nampula. Except for its proximity to Malawi on its western side, it is isolated.

When Jonas flew into Lichinga, it was with the intention of starting a new Nazarene church there. He didn't know how or where to begin. He went to the local government office and registered the Church of the Nazarene as a church that intended to establish itself in the town and in the province. He then walked through the streets of the town. As he walked, he prayed. He looked at the people as he passed them on the streets. He saw families through the windows of their homes—a father, a mother, children. People for whom Christ died. People in need of a Savior. "O God," he prayed, "help me to win these people for You. Help me to establish the Church of the Nazarene in this town of Lichinga. I don't know how to go about it. I don't know what my next move should be. Show me. Help me!"

Then, as he walked and prayed, he saw a great crowd of people. He went over and spoke to someone. What were all these people doing here? Someone had died, he was told, and the people had gathered for the funeral. Jonas went to speak to the immediate family, to offer his condolences. They appreciated his words and were moved by his concern. What about their own pastor who was to officiate at the funeral? There was no pastor. They did not know any pastor whom they could ask. "We are alone," they said. These were unchurched people—people who needed Christ.

"I am a pastor of the Church of the Nazarene," Jonas told them. "Would you like me to take the funeral service?" Yes, indeed! So Jonas took his Bible and his Nazarene *Manual* and performed this ministry of compassion.

That was how it happened. That was how, for the first time, a minister of the Church of the Nazarene preached in Lichinga. He preached a funeral sermon. His congregation had never seen him before, nor had he ever seen any of his congregation before. But "God works in mysterious ways, His wonders to perform." Jonas went back to the house the following day, to pray with the family and friends of the deceased—and 10 of them were converted to Christ. When Jonas left Lichinga, after his short visit, he left behind him a Nazarene preaching point with about a dozen people in attendance.

We now had a foothold in the Niassa province, for outreach to the Yao, Nyanja and Makua tribes.

"God opened the doors for the gospel," affirmed Jonas, "even though this is a stronghold of Islam. Many people have repented and turned to the Christian faith. We now have six churches among the Makua tribe in the region of Lichinga-Niassa. I am now looking to go to the provinces of Zambezia and Cabo Delgado."

Zambezia and Cabo Delgado were the last two provinces of the North that had yet to be entered by the Church of the Nazarene, said Jonas. But the church has since established a new work in the Zambezia province. From central Mozambique to the country's northern border, only one province remains without a Nazarene church. That situation is already changing even as these words are penned. Cabo Delgado is the final frontier.

* * *

When Mozambique missionary Dennis Riggs, accompanied by Southeast field director Ken Walker, set out to tour the work in the North, they did so by air. They went by Nazarene Mission Air, the missionary aviation service of the Church of the Nazarene in Africa. This gave him the opportunity of visiting many different centers of Nazarene activity in that vast region.

"I was impressed," reports Dennis, "by the way in which the Lord is using our Nazarenes from the South to begin our ministry in the central and northern areas. Our Nazarenes have been dispersed throughout the whole of Mozambique. Some are in government positions and in other kinds of employment. But the good news is that they are well-equipped with the gospel. They are excited about starting the work of the church in the area where they are serving.

"At first, I was concerned about how these Shangaan Nazarenes would be able to start work in an area that was culturally and linguistically different from their home area. But my fears were soon gone, as I visited church after church and saw how well-adapted they were to their local situation and culture.

"As we visited each new area, I sensed that there was an excitement about what the Lord had been doing and was going to do. It was marvelous to see how the Lord would lead a person or group to begin a new church. And the way in which these churches were growing was evidence of the leading of the Holy Spirit. In each area we met laymen who felt directed by the Lord to lead their local group until a pastor was available. And, when they finally do get a pastor, the laymen work side by side with him, to see the work go forward.

"One of the most exciting things I saw in each area was the tremendous amount of initiative the people had. They have not been waiting to see what the general church or the regional office could do for them. They have stepped out in faith. They have worked, evangelized, built churches out of mud blocks, with thatched roofs. Whether they have outside help or not, they are determined to see the work go forward."

And so it will, because God is in it.

7

The College, the Key

"The keys, if you please," demanded the government official. The keys were handed over. The doors were locked. The Nazarene Bible College on the Tavane Mission Station was closed. Nationalized. Confiscated. It was the year 1975.

But we must go back to 1973, to see the hand of God at work, because it was in that year that the Lord put into my heart the great desire to go to the capital city of Maputo (or Lourenço Marques, as it was then called) and start an extension Bible school. It was a Bible school without buildings of its own. Churches were to be used as classrooms. Part-time students would work during the day and study in the evenings. A Bible school that took the training to the students: nonresident students who would be served by a staff of traveling teachers, through a network of local study centers.

It was an immediate success. It started with 70 students and grew to over a hundred. Rev. Simeon Mandlate was my closest colleague in this new venture. But it lasted only until 1975, the Year of the Revolution. The year in which all things religious in Mozambique seemed to be falling apart. That year the keys of the Tavane Bible School were surrendered to a government official, and its doors

69

closed. In that year, too, the extension Bible school in Maputo came to an end, with the departure of the missionaries and the cutting off of mission funds.

And yet, in the providence of God, a seed had been sown that was yet to bear its finest fruit. An idea had been let loose that was yet to realize its greatest potential.

In 1981, during my first visit back to Mozambique since the revolution, a delegation of former extension students came to me in Maputo. "We want to study the Bible," they said. "We want to prepare ourselves to serve God. We want training, Bible school training. The church must restart the extension program. We need it. We really need it."

So there it was: the seed began to germinate. It was an idea whose time had come. I had not known, when I first started the extension program, that in a very short time we would lose our residence school in Tavane—the buildings, that is. But God knew. He knew what the future held. And He was already ahead of us, planning for that day, when it came, as it surely would. He gave people like Simeon Mandlate an insight into the concept of distance education, the concept of TEE—Theological Education by Extension. The concept was to have a Bible school without buildings of its own, a school without walls. Only the Lord knew the full significance of the words I wrote in my Mission Council report in 1974: "It seems that theological education by extension has come to Mozambique 'for such a time as this.'"

The new extension program opened on February 2, 1982, with Rev. Simeon Mandlate as director, Vicente Mbanze as a full-time teacher, and four part-time teachers. There were over 100 students enrolled.

* * *

Sitting on the platform at Central Church, I surveyed the great congregation that had gathered for yet another Bible college graduation in Maputo. Then I rose at the chairman's call to help with the presentation of certificates and diplomas. One by one they came. Fifteen graduates received fourth-year ministerial diplomas; 62 others received certificates—120 students in all. Extension students.

There was a lump in my throat, tears in my eyes, and pride in my heart. We had come a long way since February 1982. Ten years of sacrifice on the part of our Mozambicans have made the extension program what it is today.

*   *   *

It is evening, a typical evening at the Central Church extension center. There are about 14 different classes that meet here each evening, for four evenings a week. The students are beginning to arrive. After a hard day's work, it is difficult for many of them to get here in time for the first class at six o'clock. There is no time to go home first, no time to eat. They just leave work and head for the extension center. There is time enough to eat afterward, after the last class of the evening, that is. They should all be back home about nine or ten, I suppose.

Classrooms? There aren't any. Well, not classrooms as such. Now, this old building here is the original church building. This is where one of the first-year groups meet. A big group—too big, really, but what can you do with so many students and so few teachers? Then, over there you have another first-year group, meeting in that cement block building. There is a second-year group that meets in the old corrugated iron parsonage. Third-year classes are held in the adjoining room. The fourth-year students meet in the new church. Classes are everywhere, it seems.

Teachers teach with no equipment other than a chalkboard and chalk. They teach in a room or hall where the lighting is often very poor, in a school that has no office or administrative building that it can call its own. Students study in poor conditions, willing to sit on wooden benches for two hours at a stretch. They take notes as best they can without writing desks or tables.

71

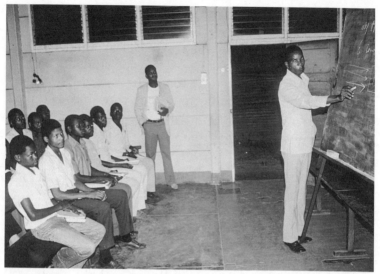

A TEE class being taught at one of the centers run by the Extension Bible School.

Motivation. That's what it's all about. Motivation of the highest order, and commitment. Commitment to Christ.

* * *

There is a serious problem that confronts the Church of the Nazarene in Mozambique. It is the urgent need for trained workers.

In Maputo the extension program has done an out-standing job in training laypeople and pastors for the churches of the Maputo District. But, because of the bush war and the disruption it has caused, extension classes in the other districts had to be discontinued at an early stage. In other words, the current extension program in Maputo serves only Maputo. No formal training has been available to the other districts since the Tavane Bible School closed in 1975. That has been a long time, too long.

The problem has been accentuated by the growth of the work in the rural areas. Churches are packed with people, among them are many new converts. They are un-churched people with no Christian background.

It is a great responsibility for the pastor who has to shepherd such a congregation: to disciple them, to nurture them, to teach them the basics of the Christian faith, to lead them to maturity in Christ, to train them in churchmanship and ministry. Who is your average pastor, upon whose shoulders rests this awesome responsibility? Certainly not an ordained minister, there are only a few of these, because of the lack of pastoral training opportunities. Who, then? Some are older preachers, who were trained as youth in the Tavane Bible School and are now ready for retirement, others are local preachers—older men—with no Bible training and may be only semiliterate. Frequently they are younger men, zealous for the Lord but with no more train-ing or education than many of their congregation.

Upon the shoulders of such men as these, faithful and true, lies the awesome task of shepherding the flock of God in the rural areas of Mozambique. In their congregations are many young people who are eager to serve God, eager for training, Bible college training.

If only we had a residence Bible college in Mozam-bique!

*   *   *

In October 1988 a proposal was made to the World Mission Division that a new residence Bible college be es-tablished in Maputo. The proposal was approved.

But a long road lay ahead; a road strewn with official red tape and bureaucracy. There were delays, endless de-lays. Then, in June 1991, District Superintendent Manuel Tshambe and I paid a crucial visit to the Executive Offices of the Maputo Council. I had the pleasure of reporting the result to our regional director, Dr. Zanner: "The concession of land for the new Bible college has been granted." At last.

Squatters were the next problem we had to deal with. There were squatters on the Bible college property. The city council would allocate another site for them and move them there. But when? There were more delays. Next, the building plans would have to be made and submitted for approval.

"Paciencia!" they say in Mozambique. "Patience! Just be patient!"

* * *

"So what do we do in the meantime?" was the question we asked ourselves. We knew that this whole building project, from planning stage to completed structure, could take a long time. The Tete District and the districts in the Gaza province were in desperate need of trained workers. The new work in the central and northeastern provinces could not afford to wait until a new Bible college was built. What were we to do?

The answer, concluded the Bible college board, was to have an interim residence program. It could be a "scaled down" program with a small number of students, living in temporary, makeshift accommodations at Central Church. They could have classes in the church and other buildings, just like the extension program does. Rev. Simeon Mandlate would head up the college. When Rev. Mandlate took a leave of absence to pursue studies toward a degree, Vicente Mbanze would become the interim principal.

So that's just what we did. We established an interim resident Bible college program at Central Church, with 20 students from the provinces, some of them couples with children.

It was a step of faith, a daring step of faith. There was no budget for such an enterprise. In the extension program we had never needed a feeding scheme; now we did. Where was the money to come from for food? Where would the money come from for textbooks, and all those other things that are needed to operate a college? Living and sleeping accommodations was severely limited, especially for couples with families. Could we really do it?

It was very hard for the students, especially at first. It was a real struggle. Adjustments had to be made by everyone. But things improved as caring Nazarenes overseas sent donations from time to time to keep the school going. But above and beyond everything else was the spirit of sacrifice displayed by the students themselves. They were just glad to be there, in Bible college, preparing themselves to serve the Lord. They were going to be able to fulfill God's call in their lives.

The program was proving so effective that, as time went on, more people wanted to come.

"I have 22 people who feel called to preach," wrote Jonas Mulate. "All of them are from central and northeastern Mozambique. They want to go to Bible college in Maputo, but the college has not yet been built. They tell us that the interim college does not have any space left to accept more students. What can we do? We are up against a brick wall. We have sown the seed. The plants are beginning to sprout. But how can we water them all without workers? These candidates, who speak different languages and represent different tribes and traditions, are anxious to study, to serve God and preach His Word. The battle for souls is being fought. But we are losing ground because we have no trained soldiers of Christ to fight it as we should. What can we do?"

What we did, in 1992, was to build some small temporary huts or shelters on the Central Church grounds. We then brought about 20 students from the North. Under pressure from other district superintendents, we accepted other candidates from the Gaza districts north of Maputo, to bring the total number of students in residence to 65. Too many students. Too little money. Too few resources.

Here is a college, if ever there was one, that has been built on faith.

* * *

"My heart says 'yes,' but my head says 'no'!"

So said Dave Restrick when he was asked about transferring from a Nazarene Bible College in South Africa to our Bible college in Maputo. His heart won.

"I didn't really know what to expect," writes Dave in a recent letter, as he recalls his first day of teaching in Maputo. "I knew conditions were going to be spartan. I had taught in other Bible colleges, but this would be a new experience—teaching in Portuguese—and when it came right down to it, I wasn't really sure what to expect.

"That first Monday when I arrived, my worst fears were confirmed. In the staff room there were no desks or chairs for teachers, no photocopier, and few supplies. In the classroom things appeared about as bad. There were only some benches and a single chalkboard standing on an easel. I thought to myself, How in the world can students learn in an environment like this? And how am I going to teach them?

"There were 17 students in that classroom. They came from various parts of Mozambique, mostly from the north. They were excited to be there. They were eager to learn; you could see it on their faces. I had had some students like that before but not a whole class! The Lord was there, almost tangibly. I began teaching. It was an acid test of my Portuguese. I was afraid they wouldn't understand me, so I kept asking them if they understood what I was saying. They responded eagerly, 'Yes, we understand you just fine. Keep going!' It was almost as if they didn't want to pause from the teaching and the learning. I wasn't used to that kind of attitude.

"I've spent three weeks with them now. And my admiration for them grows with each session we have together. I see their dedication and eagerness to learn, not just information, but to learn how to serve the Lord. They live in what we would call unacceptable conditions, yet they don't complain. Instead, they exhibit a joy and a strength that comes only through the Lord. I didn't really know what to expect, but I wasn't expecting much. Now I am expecting a great deal as the Lord works in and through the lives of the Mozambique students."

* * *

On the outskirts of the city of Maputo there is a large piece of ground. It is called Laulane, and it is the site for the proposed new Bible college—the Seminario Nazareno de Moçambique.

There are no Nazarene buildings on it yet, but there will be, soon. When the first phase of the building is completed, we will then move the interim resident students from Central Church to Laulane, leaving the extension program to carry on at Central. It will take a while, and a lot of money, but the second phase will then be built, and then the third. More students will come. People who have waited a long time for the privilege of studying to show themselves "approved unto God" (2 Tim. 2:15, KJV). Others, too, will come, until the site at Laulane will begin to fulfill its destiny as a Bible training institution of the Church of the Nazarene. There will be training for the pastors and leaders of the church, the church of today and tomorrow.

Extension students receiving their certificates and diplomas

There will be men and women who know their God; who know His Word and who preach it. There will be those who will lead a dynamic and growing church in its ministry to a great and beautiful country.

The college is the key to the future of the Church of the Nazarene in Mozambique.

* * *

As you can see, the Church of the Nazarene is on the move in Mozambique. It is alive and victorious. It has come through raging rivers without being swept away; through fire without being consumed. There is still a rough path ahead, but God knows every step. With strong faith born of adversity and tested by trials, the Mozambican Nazarenes will continue to reach their country with the gospel. Yes, "the elephants, they fight," and it is the grass that suffers, but God will provide healing and rest, and the grass will flourish again.